What's Inside the Sun?

Jane Kelly Kosek

The Rosen Publishing Group's
PowerKids Press™
New York

For Steve—one who knows the beauty of light.
Special thanks to Christopher H. Starr at the Pacific Sierra Research Corporation.

Published in 1999 by The Rosen Publishing Group, Inc.
29 East 21st Street, New York, NY 10010

First Edition

Book Design: Kim Sonsky

Photo Credits: Cover, back cover, title page, pp. 6, 7, 10, 13, 18, 21 © Digital Vision Ltd., p. 5 © FPG International/Ken Ross, p. 14 © FPG International/Telegraph Colour Library, p. 17 by Seth Dinnerman.

Kosek, Jane Kelly.
    What's inside the sun? / by Jane Kelly Kosek.
        p. cm. — (What's inside?)
    Includes index.
    Summary: Describes the six layers of the sun as well as the role
    of this star which is part of the Milky Way.
    ISBN 0-8239-5279-7
    1. Sun—Internal structure—Juvenile literature. 2. Sun—Juvenile literature.
    [1. Sun.] I. Title. II. Series: Kosek, Jane Kelly. What's inside?
    QB539.I5K68 1999
    523.7—DC21   97-43120
                                                                CIP
                                                                AC

Manufactured in the United States of America

Contents

How Did the Sun Form?

It may seem to us that the sun has been around forever. Actually, most **astronomers** (uh-STRON-uh-merz) believe the sun formed about 4.5 billion years ago. That may sound like a long time, but to astronomers who study space it's actually a short amount of time.

At first, the sun was just a huge cloud of **gas** (GAS) and dust. Eventually this cloud of gas **collapsed** (kuh-LAPSD) on itself and the sun was formed. Then, the gas and dust that was left over traveled around the sun. Later, this formed the moons and the nine planets of our **solar system** (SOH-ler SIS-tem). The nine planets are Mercury, Venus, Earth, Mars, Jupiter, Saturn, Uranus, Neptune, and Pluto.

Astronomers can study the sun to learn more about the nine planets in our solar system. ▶

Our Sun the Star

Did you know that our sun is a star, just like the stars you see in the night sky? It is one of about 300 billion stars in our **galaxy** (GAH-lik-see), which is called the Milky Way. Our sun looks different from the other stars because it is the closest star to us—even though it is 92 million miles from Earth.

A star goes through different stages in life. What a star is called depends on how old and how massive it is. As a star ages, it may be called a red giant, then a white dwarf, a supernova, and finally a black hole. Our sun is still young. It has not yet reached these later stages in a star's life.

◄ Our solar system is just a tiny part of our galaxy, the Milky Way.

A Big Ball of Gas

The sun is about 865,000 miles across. It is made of gases. This means that it is not a solid or a liquid. But something must keep all of the gases together. **Pressure** (PRESH-er) does this job. Pressure is when something pushes on something else. The sun's gases stay together because the pressure pulling gases toward the center is the same as the pressure pushing gases away from the sun's center.

The sun is made up of mostly hydrogen gas. It also contains helium and small amounts of other gases.

This X-ray picture of the sun shows that its surface is always changing. ▶

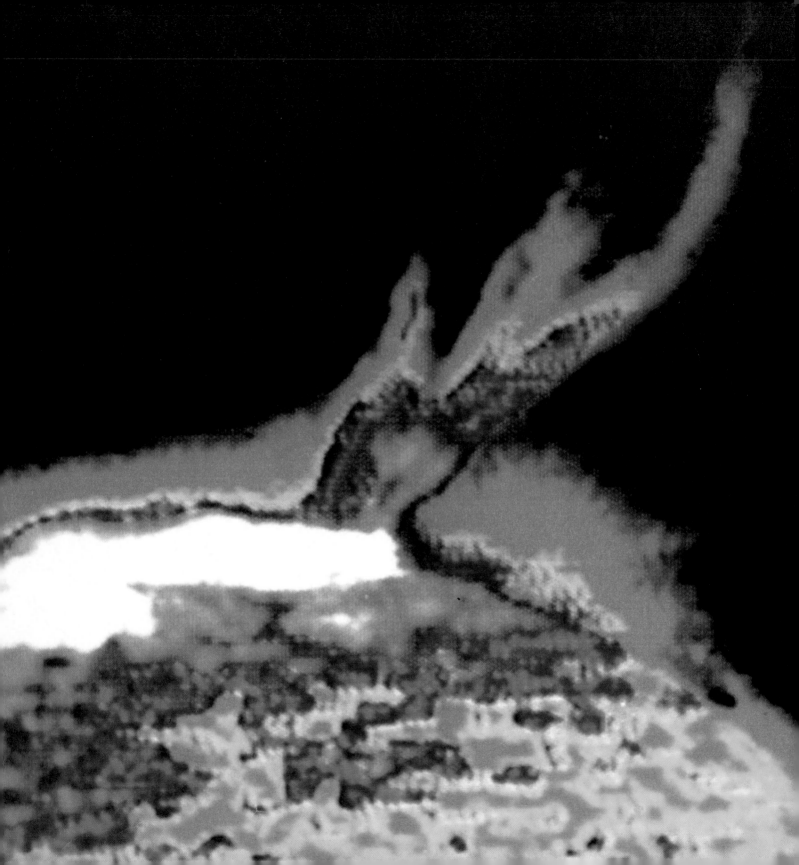

What Does the Sun Give Us?

The sun gives heat, light, and **energy** (EN-er-jee) for all living things. Without the sun, we couldn't survive. The heat and light from the sun allow plants to grow so animals and people have food to eat. Did you know that the sun gives energy to trees so they can grow, and the trees give off a gas that we need to breathe?

The sun also gives us rain. Heat from the sun causes water on Earth to **evaporate** (ee-VAP-er-ayt). This water forms the clouds we see in the sky. Then the clouds release water, which falls from the sky as rain or snow. This is the source of Earth's fresh water.

◀ The sun gives energy to green plants, which gives us energy when we eat their fruit, leaves, or roots.

How Many Layers Does the Sun Have?

The sun has six layers. The center of the sun is the **core** (KOR). The **temperature** (TEMP-rah-cher) in the sun's core is about 27 million degrees. This is the hottest part of the sun. Energy released in the sun's core moves to the sun's surface through the second and the third layers of the sun. The second layer is called the **radiative zone** (ray-dee-AY-tiv ZOHN). The third layer is called the **convective zone** (kon-VEK-tiv ZOHN). Then comes the **photosphere** (FOH-toh-sfeer), or light sphere. This is where sunlight is released. Next is the **chromosphere** (KROH-moh-sfeer), or color sphere. The last layer is called the **corona** (kuh-ROH-nah), or crown.

Some of the sun's layers can be seen in this diagram, which is called a cross section. ▶

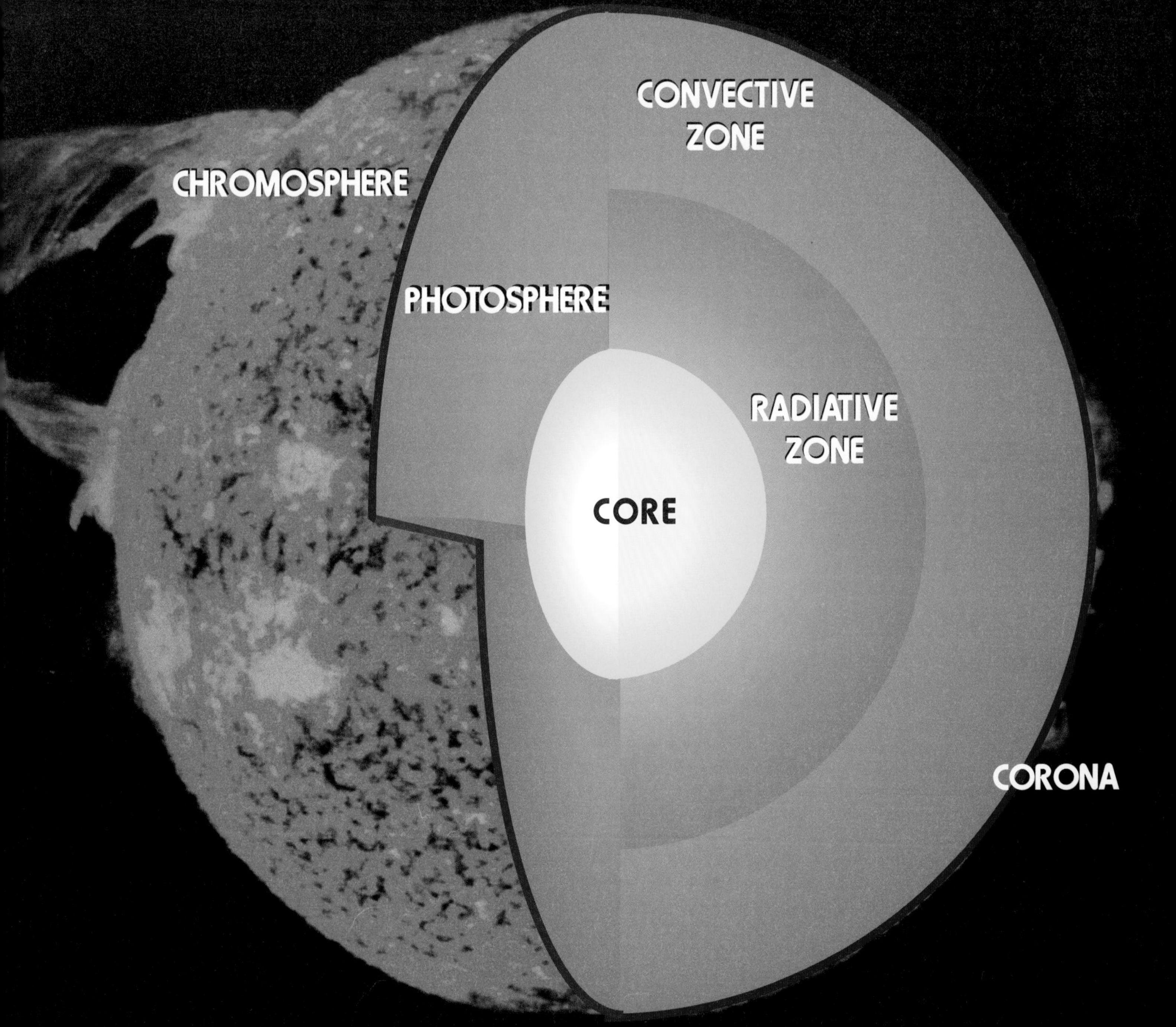
CONVECTIVE
ZONE
CHROMOSPHERE
PHOTOSPHERE
RADIATIVE
ZONE
CORE
CORONA

What Happens in the Sun's Core?

The sun's core is where all of the sun's energy is released. The sun needs energy so that it can keep living, or shine as a star. Instead of eating food to get energy, the sun gets its energy from the hydrogen in its core. Because there is so much pressure on the sun's core, the hydrogen gas fuses, or comes together, to form helium. Energy is released when helium is created. Since the sun is so large—about 100 times larger than all of the planets put together—it needs a lot of energy to live.

◀ As hydrogen is used up in the sun's core our sun will turn a red-orange color like this star in its red giant phase.

Around the Sun's Core

After the core comes the radiative zone and the convective zone. Energy that is created in the sun's core must make its way through these two zones before it reaches the photosphere and is released as sunlight. It takes hundreds of thousands of years for energy from the core to make its way through these two zones. But it only takes a few minutes, after being released, for sunlight to reach Earth. This is because light travels very fast—millions of miles per second.

You don't realize it when you're outside, but light has traveled a long way to reach you. ▶

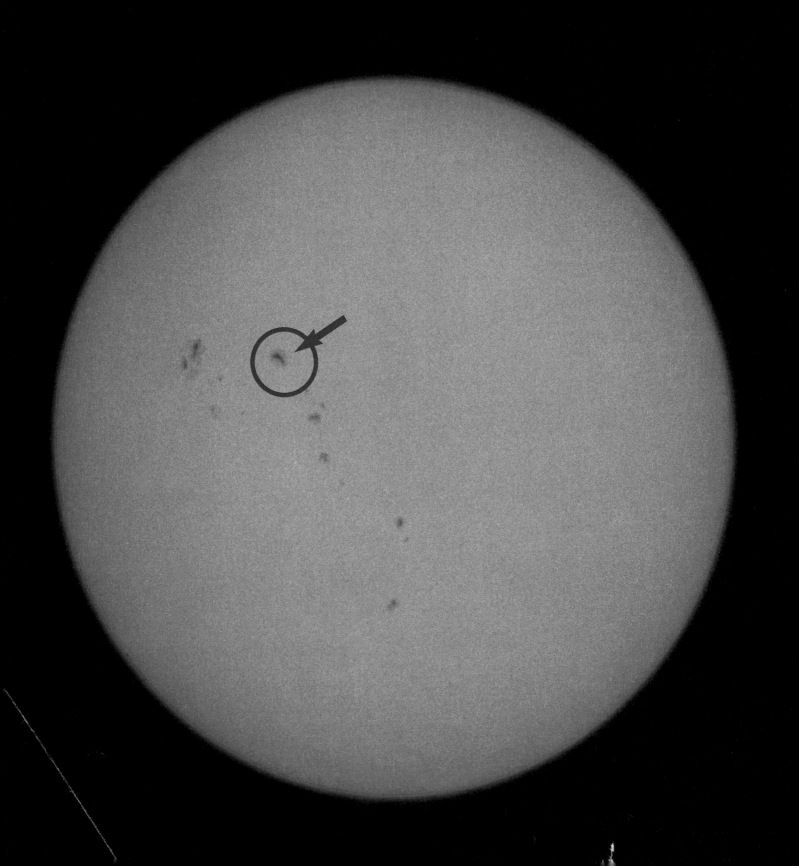

The Layer We Can See

The sunlight we see is from the layer called the photosphere, or light sphere. It is about 125 miles thick. Energy released from this layer has made the long journey from the core to the sun's surface.

The photosphere also has dark spots on it. These dark areas are called sunspots. Sunspots are darker because they are cooler than the rest of the photosphere. A sunspot only lasts for a few weeks. One early astronomer named Galileo discovered that the sun **rotates** (ROH-tayts) on its own **axis** (AK-sis) after he noticed that sunspots were constantly moving.

When the sun has a large number of sunspots, it experiences more explosions on its surface.

The Chromosphere and the Corona

The chromosphere, or color sphere, is about 2,000 miles thick and is made of **spicules** (SPIHK-yoolz), or columns of gases. Spicules make the sun's surface look like it's on fire.

The corona, or crown, is the top layer of the sun and reaches out millions of miles into space. Sometimes loops of gas will push out from the chromosphere hundreds of thousands of miles into the corona. These loops are called **prominences** (PROHM-ih-nen-sez). Solar **flares** (FLAYRZ), or explosions, in the corona release so much energy into space that if we could take that energy, we would never need another source of energy on Earth.

Some prominences travel toward the corona at 1,300 miles per second, while others stay in one place for days or even weeks. ▶

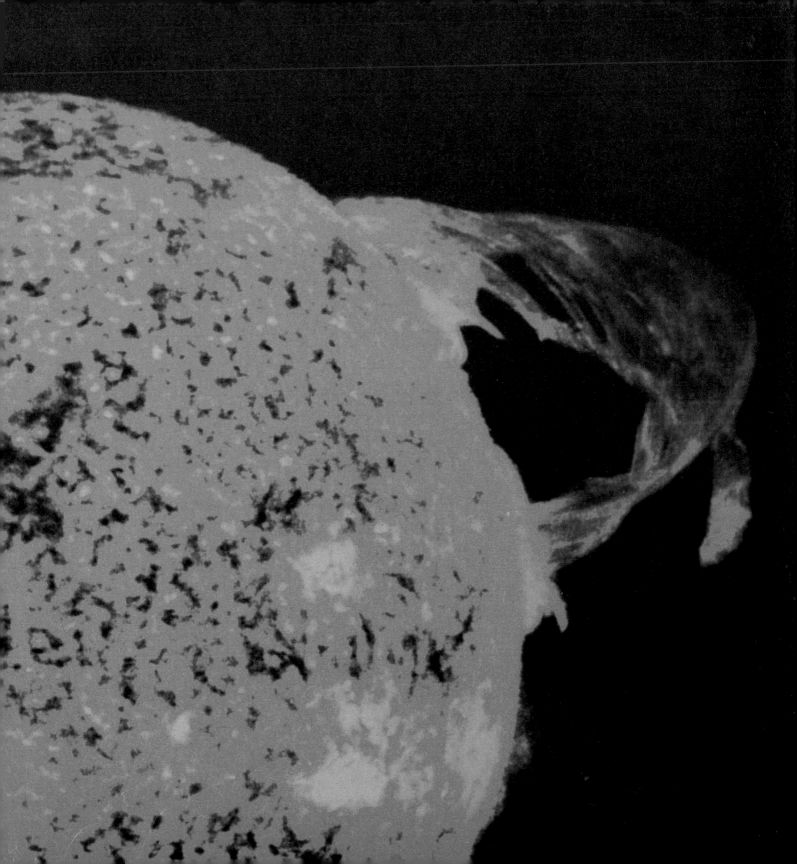

The Sun and You

The sun is more than just a big ball shining in the sky. It's full of gases and energy. Without the sun, we wouldn't have many things, including daylight or plants or animals. We rely on the sun for many things, so it's important to **respect** (re-SPEKT) the sun's power. The sun helps us, but it can also be dangerous. It gives off **ultraviolet rays** (UL-truh-VY-oh-let RAYZ), which can hurt your skin. Always wear sunscreen when you are outside in the sun. Also, do not look directly at the sun because it can harm your eyes.

As long as we remember the sun's power, we can safely enjoy its warmth and beautiful light.

Web Sites:

To learn more about the sun, check out these Web sites:
http://voyager.cs.wssu.edu/spacesci/sun.html.
http://astroa.physics.metu.edu.tr/nineplanets/sol.html

Glossary

astronomer (uh-STRON-uh-mer) A person who studies outer space.

axis (AK-sis) A straight, imaginary line on which the sun rotates.

chromosphere (KROH-moh-sfeer) The fifth layer of the sun.

collapse (kuh-LAPS) To fall down or cave in.

convective zone (kon-VEK-tiv ZOHN) The third layer of the sun.

core (KOR) The first layer, or center, of the sun where the sun's energy is released.

corona (kuh-ROH-nah) The sixth, or top, layer of the sun.

energy (EN-er-jee) Power or a source of power.

evaporate (ee-VAP-er-ayt) To change from a liquid to a gas.

flare (FLAYR) An explosion on the surface of the sun that releases a large amount of energy into space.

galaxy (GAH-lik-see) A large group of stars and the planets that circle them.

gas (GAS) A substance that is not liquid or solid.

photosphere (FOH-toh-sfeer) The fourth layer of the sun, which is the layer of the sun that we can see.

pressure (PRESH-er) A force put on something.

prominence (PROHM-ih-nens) A loop of gas that pushes out into the corona of the sun.

radiative zone (ray-dee-AY-tiv ZOHN) The second layer of the sun.

respect (re-SPEKT) To think highly of something or someone.

rotate (ROH-tayt) To move in a circle.

solar system (SOH-ler SIS-tem) The system made up of our sun, the nine planets, moons, and other space objects.

spicule (SPIHK-yool) A column of gas in the chromosphere.

temperature (TEMP-rah-cher) How hot or cold something is.

ultraviolet rays (UL-truh-VY-oh-let RAYZ) Rays given off by the sun that are dangerous to our skin and eyes.

Index